PLAYING THE GUITAR

Charlie Spencer
Illustrated by Clive Spong

Designed by Sharon Martin
Series editor: Lisa Watts

Contents

First published in 1980, in a smaller format, under the title *Beginner's Guide to Playing the Guitar.*
This edition first published in 1989 by Usborne Publishing Ltd Usborne House, 83-85 Saffron Hill London EC1N 8RT, England

Copyright © 1989, 1980 Usborne Publishing.

Printed in Belgium.

The name Usborne and the device 🜨 are Trade Marks of Usborne Publishing Limited.

How to use this book

This book is a guide to playing the guitar for absolute beginners. With colourful, step-by-step pictures it shows you how to strum and play different chords, and there are lots of songs to practise on.

As long as you know the tunes, you can play the songs in this book without being able to read music. Special charts show you which chords to play and when to strum. The musical notation for the songs is given at the end of the book. Ask someone to play the tunes you don't know and try to remember them.

Most of the pictures show Spanish or steel-strung guitars, but you can use this book to learn how to play the electric guitar, too. Pages 48–49 give some extra information about electric guitars.

Every time you play the guitar you have to make sure it is in tune. There are simple, picture-by-picture instructions which show you how to tune the guitar using a piano, pitch pipes or a tuning fork.

You may find some of the chords a bit difficult at first, but with practice your hands and fingers will become stronger, and the skin on your fingertips will harden. It takes lots of practice to get really good at the guitar.

At the back of the book there are six pages of chord charts which show you how to play over 80 chords. So if you come across a chord you do not know in other song books, you can look it up at the back of this book.

3

Types of guitar

There are two main types of guitar: acoustic and electric. Acoustic guitars have a hollow body and a sound hole. Electric guitars are solid and only make a sound when they are plugged into an amplifier and loudspeaker. Both kinds of guitar usually have six strings, but can have twelve.

Acoustic guitars

There are two types of acoustic guitar. The **classical** or **Spanish** type has nylon strings and is used mostly for classical and folk music.

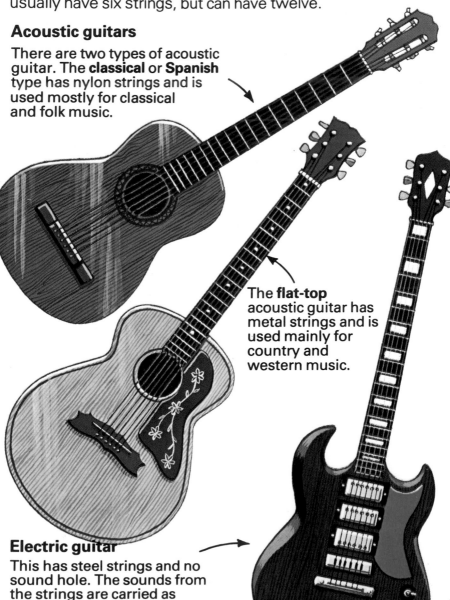

The **flat-top** acoustic guitar has metal strings and is used mainly for country and western music.

Electric guitar

This has steel strings and no sound hole. The sounds from the strings are carried as electrical signals to the amplifier, where they are changed back into sounds.*

4   *For more about electric guitars, see pages 48-49.

Choosing a guitar

The classical or Spanish guitar is the best type to learn on. The nylon strings are easier and less painful to hold down than steel strings, and it is less expensive than an electric guitar.

It is better to buy a full-sized guitar, rather than a junior one, which is really no easier to play. If possible, when you buy a guitar, take someone with you who already plays.

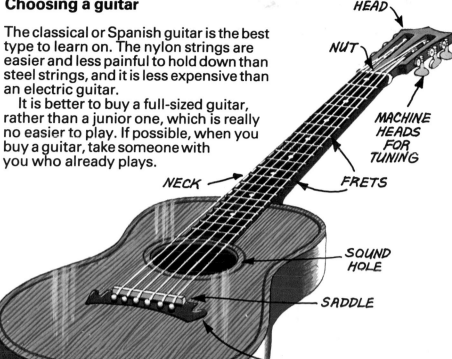

HEAD

NUT

MACHINE HEADS FOR TUNING

FRETS

NECK

SOUND HOLE

SADDLE

BRIDGE

Points to look out for

Pluck the strings to make sure the tone is good and the strings do not make a buzzing sound.

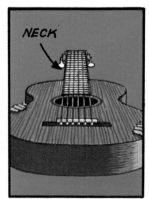

NECK

Look down the neck of the guitar from the bridge end to make sure it is not warped.

BRIDGE

Make sure the bridge is firmly glued on and the machine heads turn easily.

5

First notes and strumming

Each of the strings on the guitar makes a different sound, or note. The notes are named after the letters of the alphabet, and the strings are numbered. On a six-string guitar, the thinnest string is called the first string and the thickest string is the sixth.

Each time before you play, you have to adjust the strings to make them play the right notes. This is called tuning and is explained on pages 8–9.

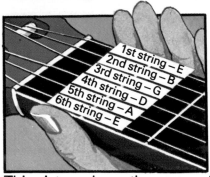

1st string – E
2nd string – B
3rd string – G
4th string – D
5th string – A
6th string – E

This picture shows the names of the strings and the notes they play. The note E made by the sixth string is lower than the first string E.

Holding the guitar

When you are learning to play, sitting down is the best position. Choose a chair without armrests, rest the guitar on your thigh and hold the neck in your left hand.

If you want to play standing up, use a shoulder strap to support the guitar.

Left-handers

Many left-handed guitarists find they can hold the guitar the same way as a right-handed person. If it is uncomfortable for you though, you can change the order of the strings, as shown on the right, so you can hold the neck in your right hand.

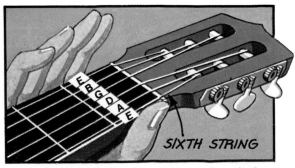

SIXTH STRING

Restring the guitar like this, so the sixth string (the thickest) is nearest you when you hold the neck of the guitar in your right hand.

How to strum

Brush your thumb down over the strings above the sound hole. Try and use equal pressure on all the strings.

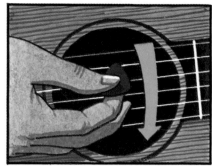

You can also strum with a piece of plastic called a pick or plectrum. This is mainly used on steel strings, but you can use it on a Spanish guitar.

If you strum the strings near the bridge, the sound is bright and crisp.

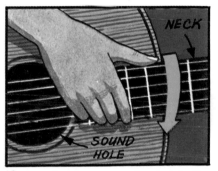

If you strum nearer the neck, the sound is much softer. The normal place to play is over the sound hole.

To change the notes made by the strings, you press them against the frets on the neck of the guitar with your other hand.

When you play a string without pressing it against a fret, it is called "playing the string open".

Playing in tune

Each time before you play the guitar you should check the strings are making the right sounds, and adjust them if necessary. This is called tuning. The sounds the strings make depend on how tight they are. Nylon strings, especially new ones, need tuning frequently because they stretch. You need a piano, or pitch pipes or a tuning fork to make the right notes to tune the strings to.

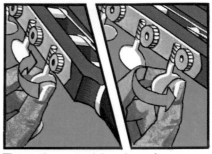

Turn the machine head clockwise to tighten a string and make the sound higher, and anti-clockwise to loosen it and make the sound lower.*

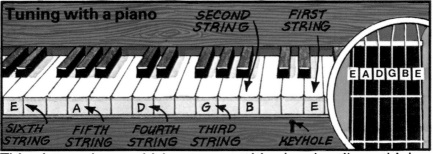

Tuning with a piano

SECOND STRING   FIRST STRING

E A D G B E

E   A   D   G   B   E

SIXTH STRING   FIFTH STRING   FOURTH STRING   THIRD STRING   KEYHOLE

This picture shows which notes you should play for each of the guitar strings. Play one of the piano notes, then pluck the guitar string for that note. Listen carefully and adjust the machine head until you think the string makes the same sound as the piano. Tune all the strings, then check them as shown opposite.

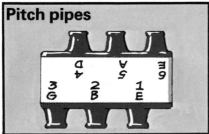

Pitch pipes

Each pipe makes the sound of the note marked on it. Blow down one of the pipes, then tune the string for that note to the sound made by the pipe.

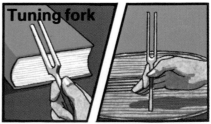

Tuning fork

You need a tuning fork which makes the note bottom E. Hit the fork on something, not too hard, then hold it on the guitar. Pluck the sixth string and tune until it sounds like the tuning fork. Tune the other strings as shown on the right.

8   *The machine heads turn in different directions on steel-strung acoustic guitars, see page 51.*

Tuning the strings to each other

The notes E, A, D, G, B, E made by the open strings, can also be played by pressing certain strings at different frets. To check the strings are in tune with each other, you should play each string open, and make sure the sound is the same as when you play that note on one of the other strings, as shown below.

If you tune the sixth string with a tuning fork, you have to use this method to tune all the other strings.

To make note A, the sound of the fifth string, press the sixth string just behind the fifth fret. Pluck the string with your other hand.

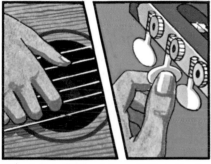

Pluck the fifth string. If it sounds different from the sixth string, turn the machine head to raise or lower the sound.

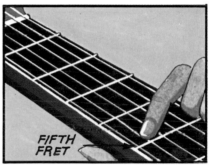

Now press the fifth string at the fifth fret and pluck it to play D. Pluck the fourth string and tune it if it sounds different.

Press the fourth string at the fifth fret and tune the third string to it.

Press the third string at the fourth fret and tune the second string to it.

Press the second string at the fifth fret and tune the first string to it.

First chords

A chord is a group of notes played together. Different chords are made up of different groups of notes, and each chord is named after one of the notes in the group.

To play chords on the guitar you press the strings against the frets to make different notes, and strum the strings with your other hand. These two pages show you how to play the chord of G.

How to make G chord

First, to help you follow the pictures, it is a good idea to number your fingers with a felt-tip pen, as shown above.

Hold the neck of the guitar between your thumb and first finger and tilt it towards you so you can see the strings.

SECOND FRET

Press the fifth string just behind the second fret with your first finger. Make sure the finger does not touch other strings.

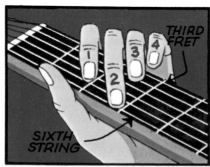

THIRD FRET

SIXTH STRING

Put your second finger on the sixth string, just behind the third fret, and press down hard.

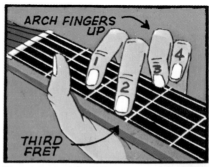

ARCH FINGERS UP

THIRD FRET

Put your third finger on the first string, just behind the third fret. Each finger should touch only the string it is supposed to.

Strumming the chord

PRESS HARD HERE

Keep pressing the strings hard against the frets, and with your other hand, brush your thumb down across the strings over the sound hole.

Make sure you strum all the strings evenly. If the notes sound dull, check you are doing all the things shown below.

RIDGES

Make sure your fingers are just behind the fret ridges, and not on top of them.

Press the strings really hard, pressing from behind with your thumb too.

Arch your fingers up over the strings so they do not touch any they are not supposed to.

Chord charts

In this book there are lots of charts like this which show you how to play different chords. The chart shows the neck of the guitar, with the nut on the left. The thick, black, vertical lines are the frets and the thinner lines across the chart are the strings. String six is nearest you, like it is when you hold the guitar. The red circles with numbers show you which fingers to use and where to put them.

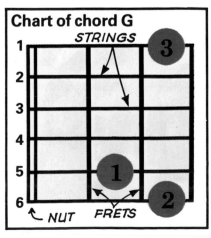

Chart of chord G

STRINGS

3

1

2

NUT   FRETS

1 2 3 4 5 6

11

Keeping time

Most songs have a regular beat running through them, and you have to strum in time with this beat. Try strumming the chord of G to a regular beat of "one, two, three, four" repeated lots of times. This is called "four-time". To help you keep time you can count out loud at first, and most musicians also tap their foot in time with the beat.

Sit comfortably holding the guitar and count "one, two, three, four", out loud. Tap with your foot at the same time.

With your fingers in position for chord G (shown on the right), keep counting, and on each count, strum the strings.

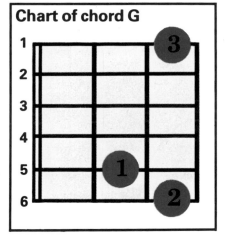

Chart of chord G

Practice chart

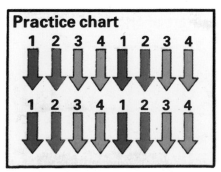

This is a chart to help you keep time. Count "one, two, three, four", and strum the strings once for each of the arrows.

Sore fingers

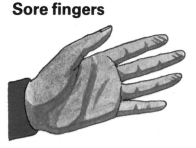

Your fingers pressing the strings will probably get quite sore at first. To help the skin on the tips harden, rub it with surgical spirit from a chemist.

How to play chord C

Chord C is often in the same songs as G, so this is the next chord to learn. Put your first finger on the second string behind the first fret.

Put your second finger on the fourth string, just behind the second fret. Arch your finger so it does not touch other strings.

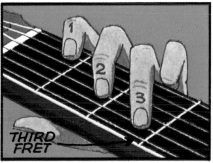

The third finger goes on the fifth string, just behind the third fret. Press hard with all three fingers.

Strum the strings over the sound hole with your other hand. If the notes sound dull, press your fingers harder on the neck of the guitar.

Practice chart

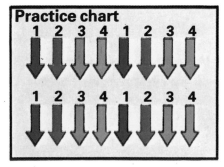

Here is a chart to practise strumming C chord. Count "one, two, three, four", and strum once for each arrow.

Chart of chord C

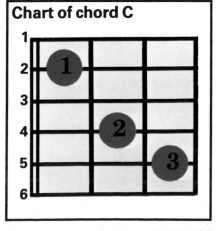

13

Changing chords

Once you know how to form G and C chords, you can play the chorus of "Mull of Kintyre". First, though, practise changing from one chord to the other on the practice chart below.

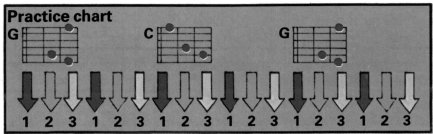

This chart is in three-time, so you count "one, two, three, one, two, three". Count very slowly at first, so you have time to change chords without missing a beat.

Mull of Kintyre

This chart shows you how to play the chorus of "Mull of Kintyre". The chord charts show which chords to play and how to position your fingers, and the arrows show you when to strum. The song is in three-time, so count "one, two, three". To play the rest of the song, given on pages 16–17, you need to learn chord D, shown opposite.*

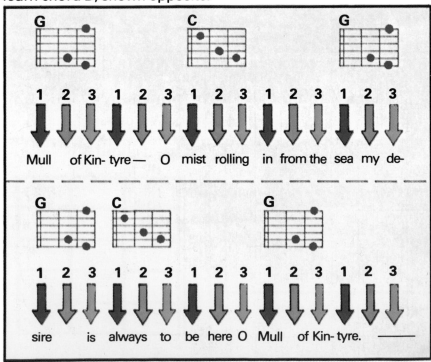

*The music for this song is on page 54.

How to play D chord

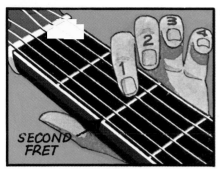

Press your first finger on the third string, just behind the second fret.

Put your second finger on the first string, just behind the second fret.

Put your third finger on the second string, behind the third fret. Press all three strings down hard.

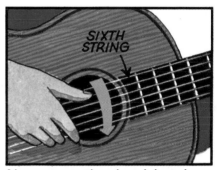

Now strum the chord, but do not touch the sixth string as that note is not part of chord D.

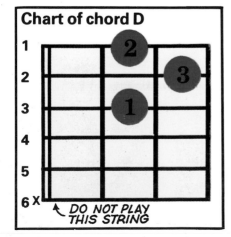

Chart of chord D

Practice chart

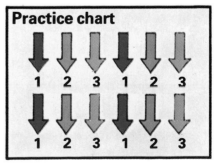

Here is a chart for you to practise strumming the chord D in three-time. Try to keep your strumming even and regular.

More about strumming

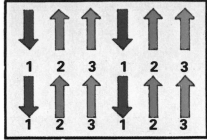

Try strumming the strings upwards, towards you. If you strum alternately up and down, it makes strumming sound lighter and more lively.

You can practise on this chart. Put your fingers in position for any chord and count "one, two, three". Strum down on "one" and up on "two, three".

Mull of Kintyre

Now you can play the rest of "Mull of Kintyre", using the new chord D and strumming up and down. Count "one, two, three" and strum down on "one" and up on "two, three", as shown by the arrows. After each verse play the chorus on page 14, strumming upwards and downwards in the same rhythm as here.

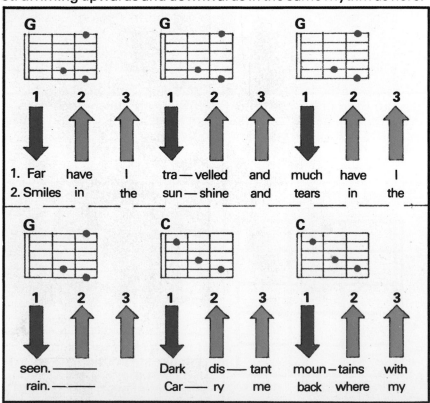

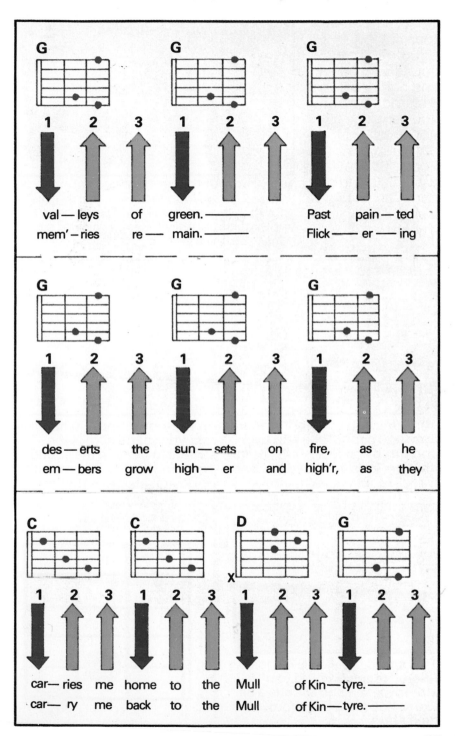

New rhythms

Regular three- or four-time strumming can sound very heavy and rigid. To give it a bit more rhythm you can put a quick upwards strum between the beats. You can also try not playing on some beats to give a slightly jerky rhythm.

Four-time with upstrokes

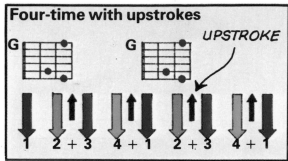

Tap your foot to four-time and count "one, two and three, four and". The word "and" is shown by a + sign. It should come between two taps of your foot. Each time you say "and", strum upwards.

Four-time missing beats

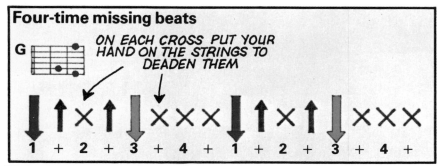

ON EACH CROSS PUT YOUR HAND ON THE STRINGS TO DEADEN THEM

This time, tap your foot to four-time and count "one and two and three and four and". Strum only on "one and" and on "and three", doing quick upstrokes on the word "and". In between, rest your hand across the strings to deaden the sound. The song "In the Summertime", opposite, uses this rhythm.

New chord

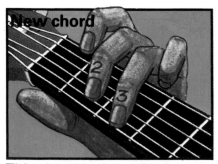

This chord is called G7. It is related to the G chord you already know and sounds a bit like it. You need this chord in the next song.

Chord chart of G7

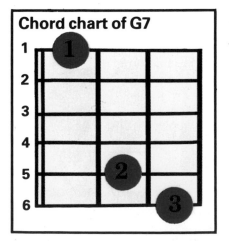

In the Summertime

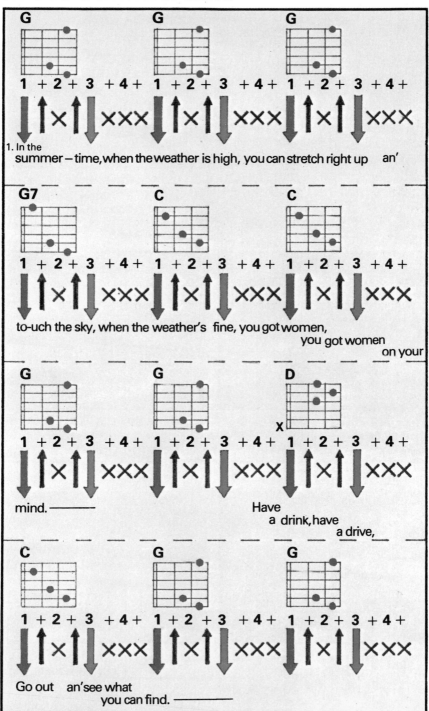

1. In the
summer – time, when the weather is high, you can stretch right up   an'

to-uch the sky, when the weather's fine, you got women,
you got women
on your

mind. ———   Have
a drink, have
a drive,

Go out   an'see what
you can find. ———

The music for this song is on page 55.   19

Minor chords

The three chords G, C and D that you know so far are called major chords. Minor chords* have a slightly sadder sound than major chords. Below you can find out how to play three minor chords, and another new chord, called A7, which you need for the next song.

These minor chords, and the major chords you already know, are all related and belong to a group called a key. The key is named after the main chord in the group.

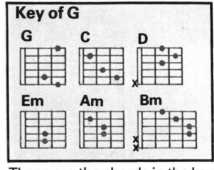

These are the chords in the key of G. The chords of one key are often found in the same song as they sound good together.

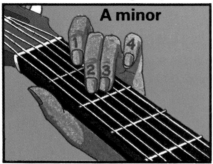

Position your fingers like this for the chord of A minor. Look at the chart in the first picture to check they are in the right places.

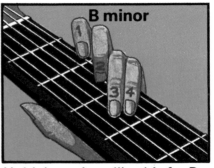

Hold the strings like this for B minor and strum only the first four strings. Do not strum the fifth and sixth strings (the two nearest you).

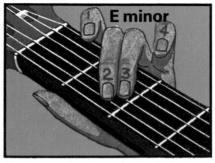

For this chord, press only the fourth and fifth strings, but strum all of them.

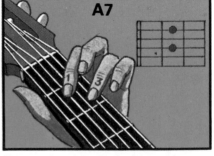

Press the two strings as shown above, and strum all the strings. This chord is not part of the key of G.

*A small "m" after the name of a chord shows it is a minor chord.

Puff (the Magic Dragon)

This song has lots of chord changes, so play it through very slowly first. It is in four-time, and you should count "one, two and three, four and", playing a quick upstroke on "and".*

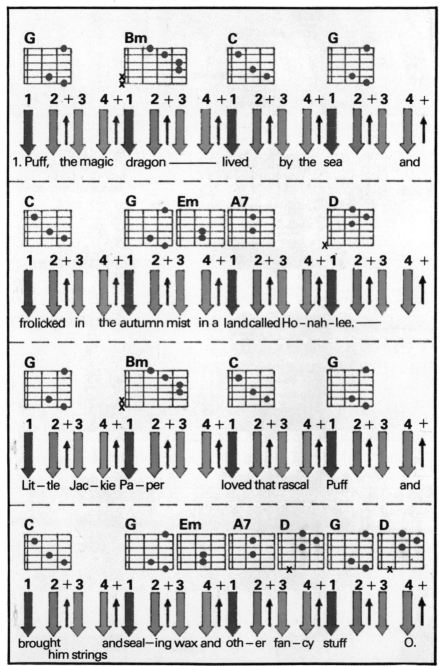

The music for this song is on page 55.

Picking and strumming

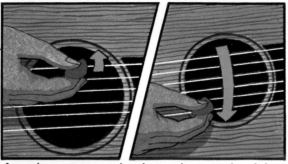

Another way to play is to alternately pick and strum the strings. Pick the string with your thumb, or plectrum, then follow with a downwards strum. You can pick the string upwards or downwards.

In this book, an arrow like this means pick the string. The number shows which string to pick.

Picking and strumming practice charts

This chart is in four-time, so count "one, two, three, four". Pick the string on the first beat, then strum three times.

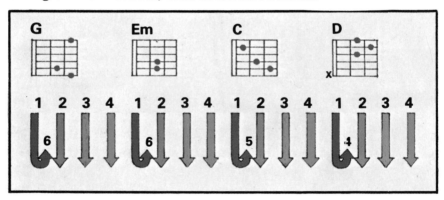

The chart below is also in four-time. but this time you alternately pick and strum the strings.

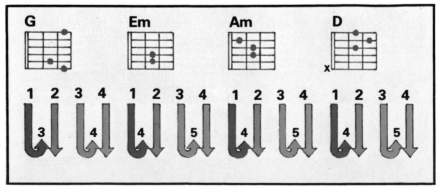

Mr Tambourine Man

You can try picking and strumming in this song by Bob Dylan. It is in four-time, so count "one, two, three, four", and pick and strum on alternate beats. The rest of the song is on pages 24–25. Play it through very slowly at first, trying to keep the beat regular.*

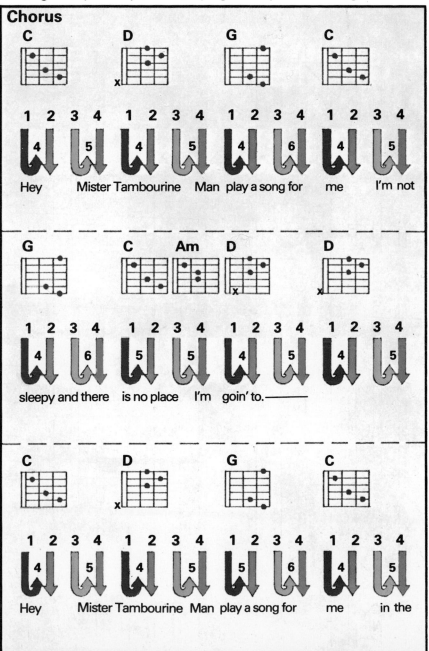

The music for this song is on page 58.

Mr Tambourine Man

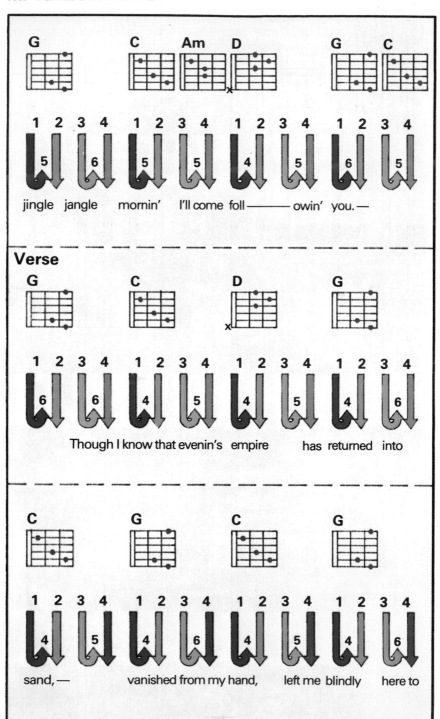

G   C   Am   D   G   C

jingle   jangle   mornin'   I'll come foll————owin' you.——

Verse

G   C   D   G

Though I know that evenin's empire   has returned into

C   G   C   G

sand,——   vanished from my hand, left me blindly here to

24

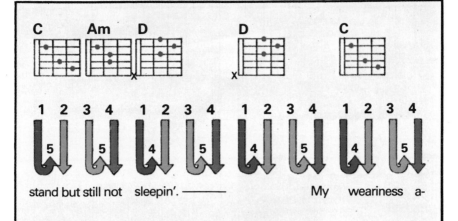

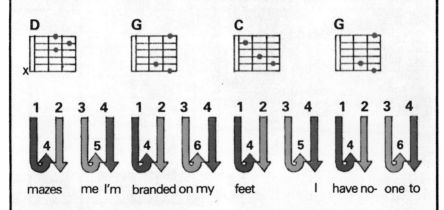

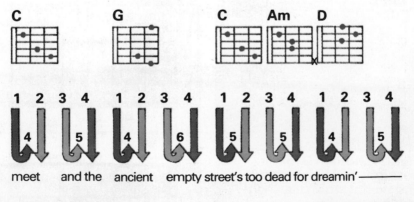

Repeat chorus

Another key

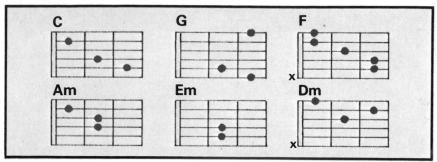

These are the chords in the key of C. Some of them are also in the key of G, shown on page 20. Chords F and Dm are new and they are shown in more detail below. Try playing the chords one after the other. They are all related and sound good together.

Position you fingers like this and do not strum the sixth string. If you find it difficult at first, you can miss out the fifth string and play only the top four.

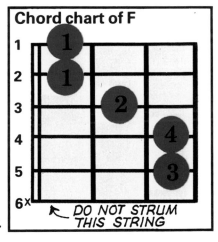

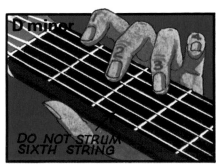

For the chord of D minor, position your fingers like this and do not strum the sixth string.

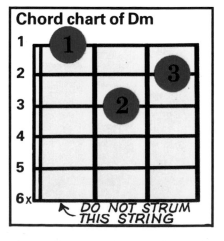

Sailing

This song by Gavin Sutherland is written in the key of C. That is, it uses most of the chords in the key of C. It is in four-time with quick upstrokes between the beats, so you count "one, two and three, four and".*

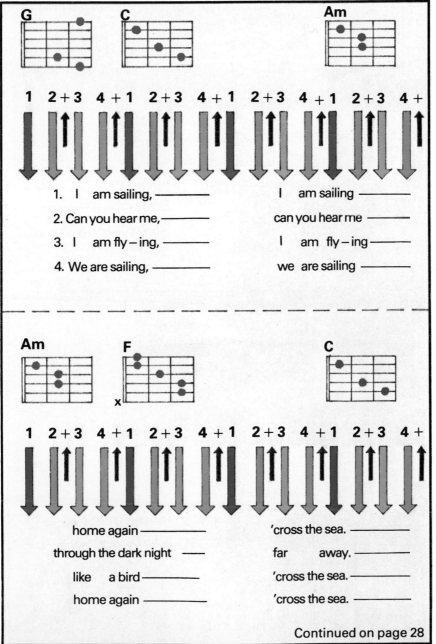

1 2 + 3 4 + 1 2 + 3 4 + 1 2 + 3 4 + 1 2 + 3 4 +

1. I   am sailing, ———   I   am sailing ———
2. Can you hear me, ———   can you hear me ———
3. I   am fly – ing, ———   I   am fly – ing ———
4. We are sailing, ———   we are sailing ———

1 2 + 3 4 + 1 2 + 3 4 + 1 2 + 3 4 + 1 2 + 3 4 +

home again ———   'cross the sea. ———
through the dark night ——   far   away. ———
like   a bird ———   'cross the sea. ———
home again ———   'cross the sea. ———

Continued on page 28

*The music for this song is on page 54.

27

Sailing

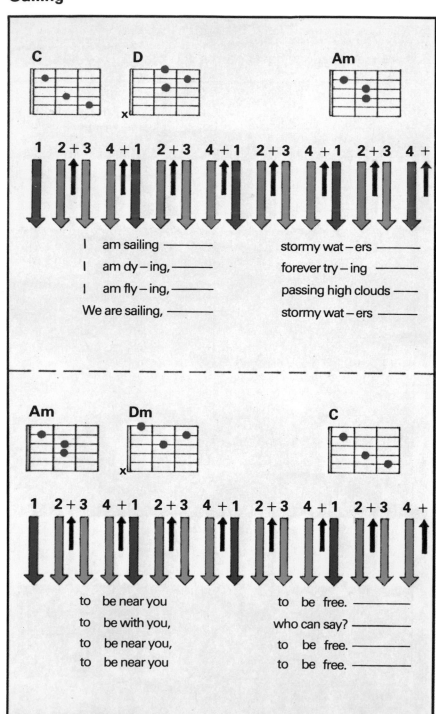

C   **D**   **Am**

1 | 2 + 3 | 4 + 1 | 2 + 3 | 4 + 1 | 2 + 3 | 4 + 1 | 2 + 3 | 4 +

I am sailing ———	stormy wat – ers ———
I am dy – ing, ———	forever try – ing ———
I am fly – ing, ———	passing high clouds ——
We are sailing, ———	stormy wat – ers ———

Am   **Dm**   **C**

1 | 2 + 3 | 4 + 1 | 2 + 3 | 4 + 1 | 2 + 3 | 4 + 1 | 2 + 3 | 4 +

to be near you	to be free. ———
to be with you,	who can say? ———
to be near you,	to be free. ———
to be near you	to be free. ———

Changing key

If you find a song is too high for you to sing, or too low, you can change all the chords for the equivalent chords of another key.

The easiest way to do this is with a capo. This is a clamp which fits round the neck of the guitar. When it is in place it automatically changes the sounds of all the chords you play to those of another key.

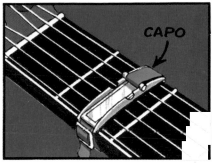

With the capo clamped round the neck of the guitar, all the strings are shorter so the sounds they make are higher.

Try clamping the capo round the second fret, and form chord C. With the capo on, count the first fret above the capo as fret one.

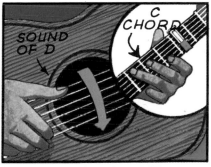

Now strum the chord. The sounds will be the notes of the chord of D, even though your fingers are in position for chord C.

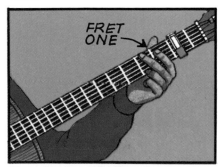

Try playing "Sailing" with the capo at the second fret. Play the chords as shown in the song on pages 27–28, counting the first fret above the capo as fret one.

With the capo, the chords C, F, G, Am, D, and Dm in "Sailing", become D, G, A, Bm, E and Em. These are the chords in the key of D, so you have changed key.

Bass runs

These are series of single notes played between two chords. Bass runs are used a lot in country and western music. You can try out some bass runs in the practice chart below. The flicked-up arrows show when to pick the strings and the number beside each arrow shows which string to pick. The chord charts above show which strings to press, and on charts with no red dots, none of the strings are pressed.

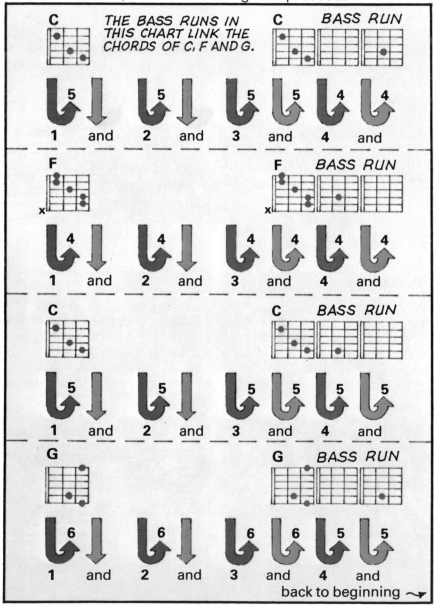

back to beginning

30

More bass runs

Here are four more bass runs linking different pairs of chords in the key of C. You could try playing "Sailing" (pages 27–28) using these runs between the chords, or you could make up your own.

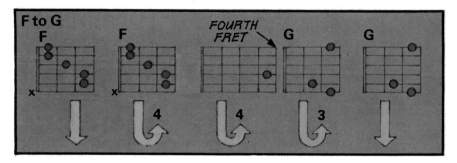

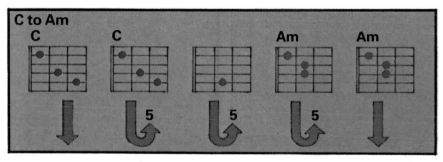

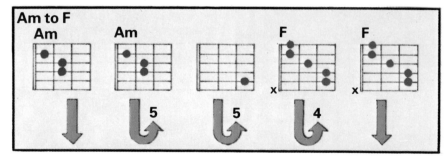

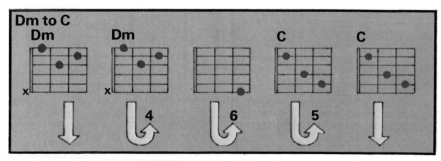

Fingerpicking

Another way of playing is to pick the strings and not to strum at all. This technique is used a lot in folk music. You need strong, long nails on your strumming hand for fingerpicking. If your nails are not strong enough, you can buy fingerpicks from a music shop.

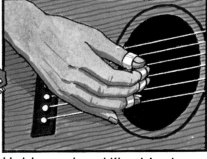

FINGER-PICKS

Fingerpicking is quite easy if you make sure you pick each string with the correct finger, as shown below.

Fingerpicks go on your first, second and third fingers, and thumb like this.

How to sit

For fingerpicking it is best to sit like this, with one foot raised on a stool or box and the guitar resting on your thigh.

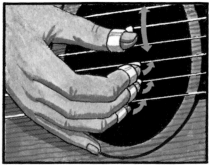

Hold your hand like this above the sound hole with your wrist arched over the strings. Rest your little finger on the guitar.

Pick each string with the correct finger – third finger for first string, second for second string, first for third string and thumb for strings four, five and six.

Fingerpicking practice

You can practise fingerpicking the tunes given in these two charts. The numbers with the flicked-up arrows show which strings to pick. The first tune is in the key of C in three-time and the second is in the key of G in four-time.

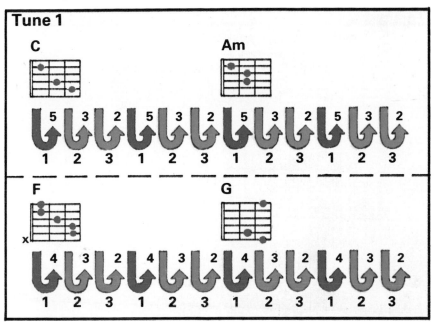

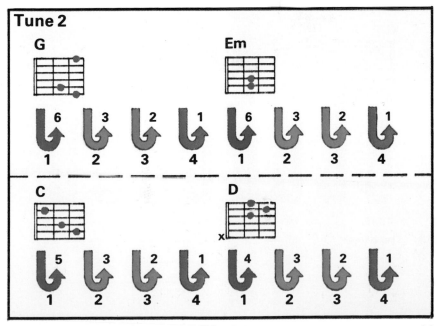

Michael Row the Boat Ashore

This is a traditional folk song that you can play by fingerpicking. It in four-time in the key of C. Play it through very slowly first, trying to keep the rhythm regular.*

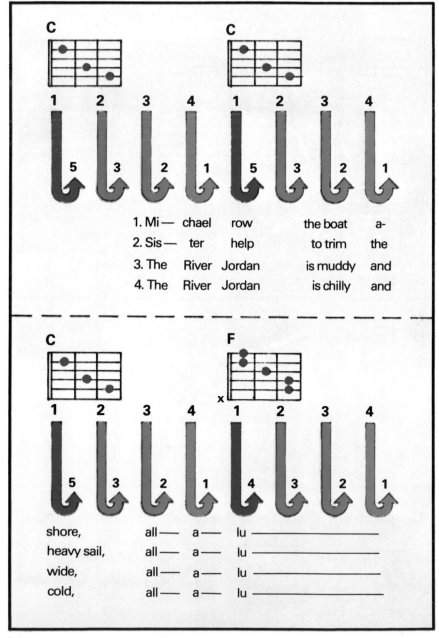

	1. Mi —	chael	row	the boat	a-
	2. Sis —	ter	help	to trim	the
	3. The	River	Jordan	is muddy	and
	4. The	River	Jordan	is chilly	and

shore,	all —	a —	lu ———————
heavy sail,	all —	a —	lu ———————
wide,	all —	a —	lu ———————
cold,	all —	a —	lu ———————

*The music for this song is on page 58.

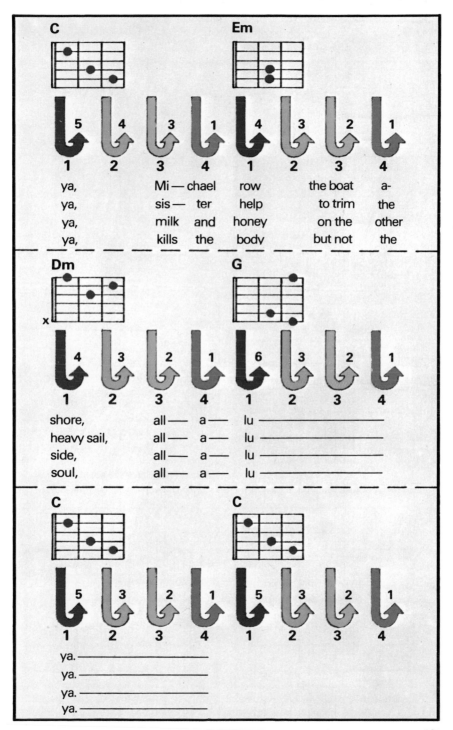

More chords

The finger positions for certain chords, such as E and A, can be used on other frets to make new chords. Chords E and A are called moveable chords.

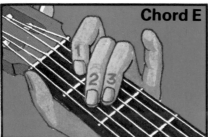

Chord E

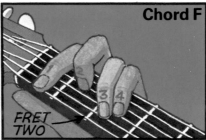

Chord F

These are the finger positions for the chord of E. Chord F, shown on the right, has the same finger positions, but moved up a fret. Also, the first finger is pressing all the strings

across the first fret, like a capo. Chords formed like this are called barré chords. In this version of chord F you play all six strings.

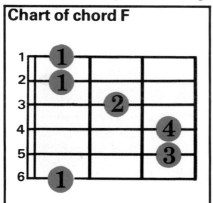

Chart of chord F

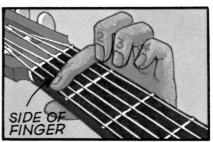

Make sure you press the strings firmly with your first finger. Use the side of the finger and press hard with your thumb behind the neck of the guitar.

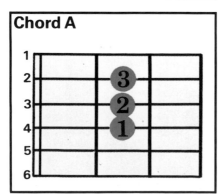

Chord A

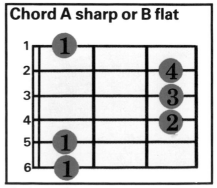

Chord A sharp or B flat

This is the moveable chord A which becomes the barré chord

A sharp (A♯) shown above. A♯ is the same as B flat (B♭).*

*The sign ♯ means sharp and ♭ means flat.

F minor

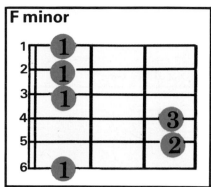

A sharp minor or B flat minor

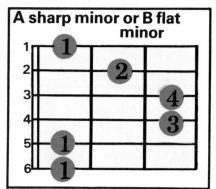

This is the barré chord of F minor. It is based on the chord of Em which you already know.

A sharp minor (A♯m) can also be called B flat minor (B♭m). It is based on the chord of Am.

Practice chart

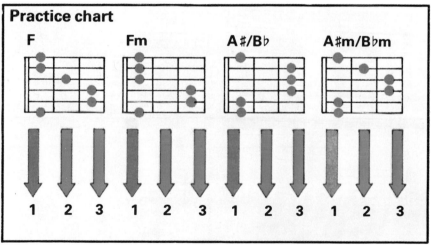

These chords sound quite good together and you can practise them by playing them in sequence.

Strum each chord three times, or work out your own strumming pattern.

Chord A♭

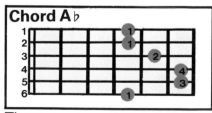

Chord D♭

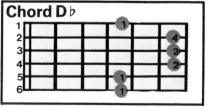

These are two more barré chords that you need for the next song "House of the Rising

Sun". A♭ is based on the E chord and D♭ is made with the A chord.

The House of the Rising Sun

This song has lots of barré chords. If you find them very hard, you need only play the top four strings of each chord. Playing all six strings, though, gives a fuller sound. The song is in six-time with a quick upstroke between beats two and three. You can pick or strum the strings on beats four, five, six.*

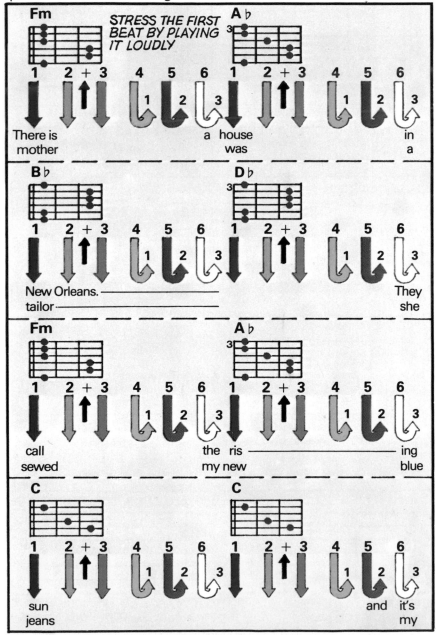

*A small number to the left of a chord chart shows which fret the chart begins at. The music for this song is on page 56.

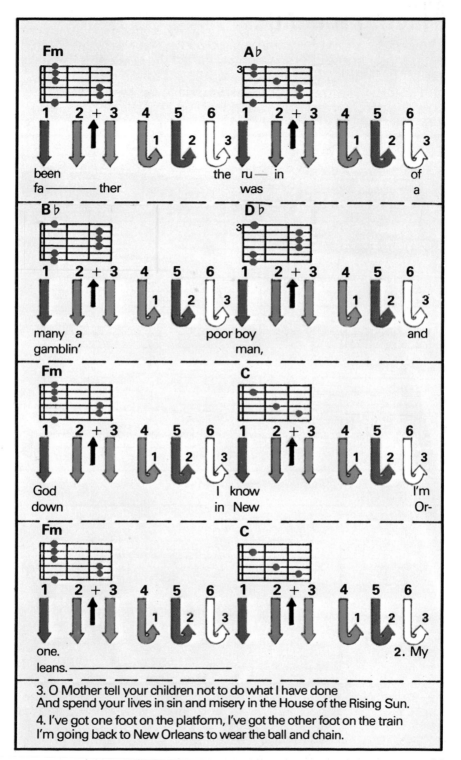

3. O Mother tell your children not to do what I have done
And spend your lives in sin and misery in the House of the Rising Sun.

4. I've got one foot on the platform, I've got the other foot on the train
I'm going back to New Orleans to wear the ball and chain.

Playing the blues

The chords shown below are used a lot in blues music. With each major chord there is a chord called the sixth and the seventh. Sixths and sevenths are related to the major chords and sound very like them. Once you have mastered these chords you can make up your own blues music, or try out the blues sequence on the right.

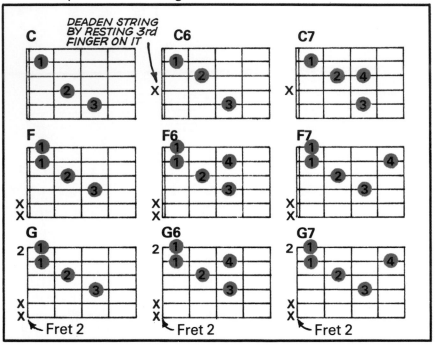

Practice chart

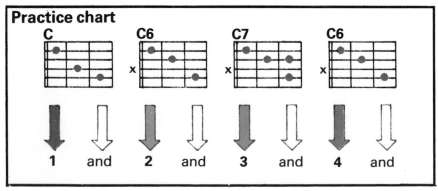

Try strumming through the C chords as in this chart, and listen to how similar they sound. Note that in C7 you leave your third finger in position so you can quickly change back to C6. You can play through the F and G chords like this too.

Twelve-bar blues

Now try playing through this blues sequence. It is in four-time and there is a quick upstroke between the count of "four" and "and".

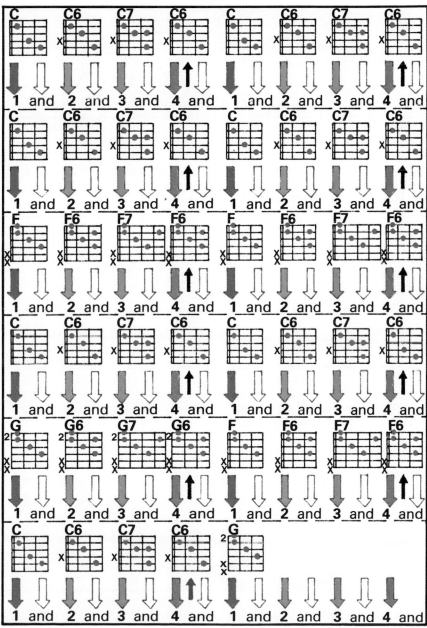

You can play it through in a fast, rocky way to give a rhythm and blues style like that of Chuck Berry, or more slowly in the mournful blues style of St James' Infirmary. If you feel like it you can make up words as well.

Special effects

Here are some special ways of playing chords and notes that you can use in songs to make them more interesting.

Hammering on

This is a way of making two sounds while playing the strings once. Pick the fourth string, then very quickly hammer your finger down on the fourth string at the second fret. The sound will go from D to E. You can "hammer on" any note or string, and chords too. Try playing the strings open, then hammer down the chord E or A.

Pulling off

Position your fingers for the chord of D and put your fourth finger on the first string at the third fret. Strum the chord, then immediately lift your fourth finger and "twang" the first string with it at the same time.

Staccato

This makes the notes sound sharp and abrupt. Choose a chord and hold your fingers lightly on the strings. Then strum, and at the same time press your fingers down hard on the strings on the neck of the guitar and release them immediately. Keep on strumming and pressing the strings like this. This style is used a lot in rock music.

Glissando

This effect is made by sliding your fingers up or down the strings between two notes or chords. Put your first finger on the first string at the third fret. Pick the string over the sound hole, then slide your finger up to the tenth fret, pressing hard.

Vibrato

SHAKE FINGER AND HAND

You can make a note sound for longer and give it a fuller sound by pressing the string down very hard and shaking your finger and hand from side-to-side.

Bending

PUSH STRING TOWARDS YOU

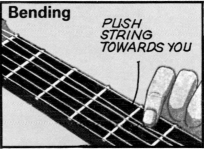

Press the second string at the fifth fret and pick it. Then push the string towards you on the neck of the guitar and the sound of the string will slide up a note.

Harmonics

These are notes with a clear, bell-like sound. Lay your fourth finger very lightly over all the strings right on the ridge of the twelfth fret.

PRESS VERY LIGHTLY

Then pick or strum the strings. You can play notes which sound like this by pressing any of the strings very lightly at the fifth, seventh or twelfth fret.

Hotel California

You can try out lots of special effects in this song, which was sung by The Eagles. It is in four-time with a quick upstroke between beats two and three. Do not strum on the fourth beat and deaden the strings by resting your hand on them. This song should be played in a short, sharp staccato style, as described on page 42.

There are four verses and two choruses. Sing the first two verses, then the first chorus which is on pages 46–47. Then sing verses four and five which are at the top of page 46. You may find it easier to copy down the words and keep the book open here for the chords. Sing the second chorus after the fourth verse.*

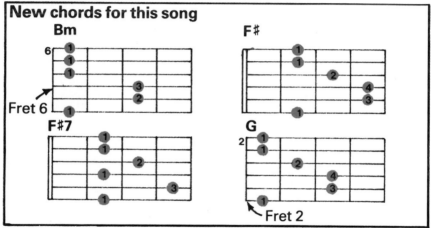

New chords for this song

Here are the finger positions for the new chords – F# and F#7, and also new ways of fingering two chords you already know – G and Bm. There are several ways of fingering all chords, and each position gives the chord a slightly different tone.

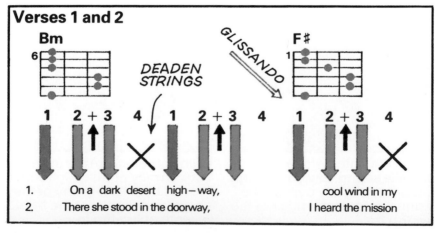

Verses 1 and 2

| 1. | On a dark desert high – way, | cool wind in my |
| 2. | There she stood in the doorway, | I heard the mission |

Music for this song is on pages 56–57.

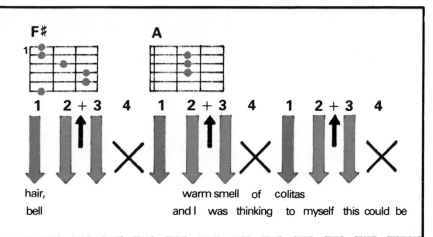

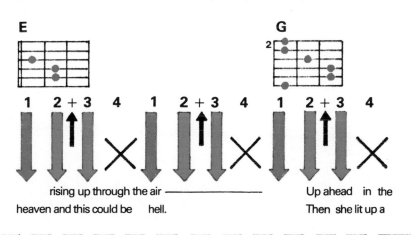

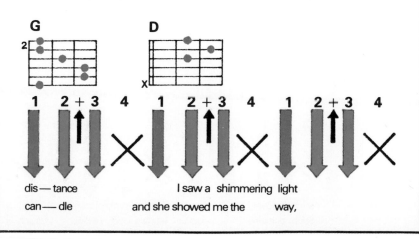

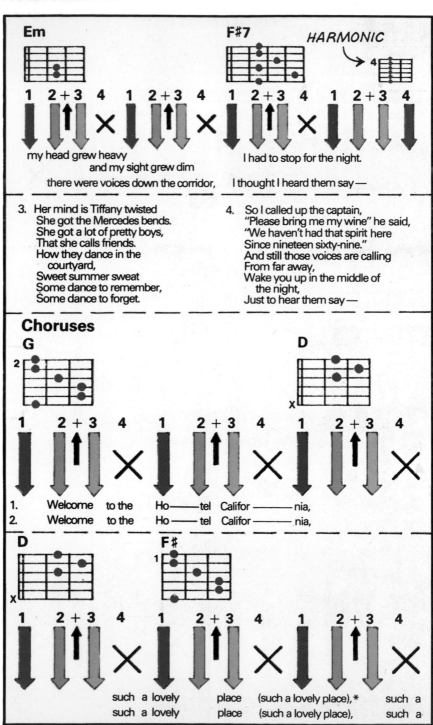

my head grew heavy
and my sight grew dim
there were voices down the corridor,

I had to stop for the night.

I thought I heard them say —

3. Her mind is Tiffany twisted
   She got the Mercedes bends.
   She got a lot of pretty boys,
   That she calls friends.
   How they dance in the
      courtyard,
   Sweet summer sweat
   Some dance to remember,
   Some dance to forget.

4. So I called up the captain,
   "Please bring me my wine" he said,
   "We haven't had that spirit here
   Since nineteen sixty-nine."
   And still those voices are calling
   From far away,
   Wake you up in the middle of
      the night,
   Just to hear them say —

Choruses

1. Welcome to the Ho——tel Califor————nia,
2. Welcome to the Ho——tel Califor————nia,

such a lovely place (such a lovely place),* such a
such a lovely place (such a lovely place), such a

46 *"Back-up" person should sing words in brackets.*

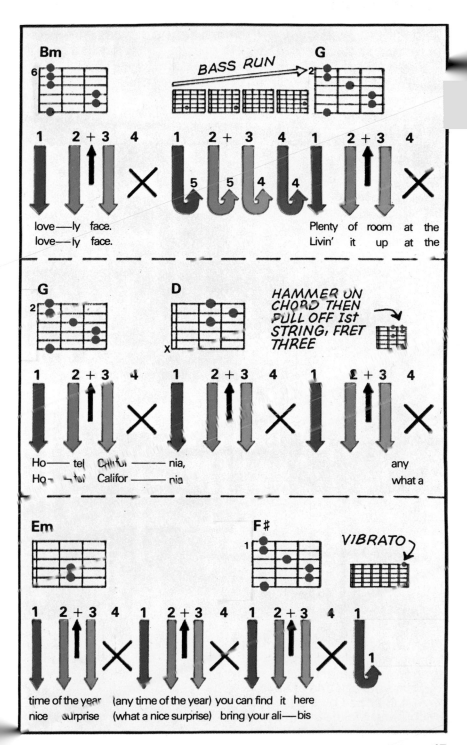

Electric guitars

All the chords and songs in this book can be played on an electric guitar just as well as on a Spanish or classical, or acoustic guitar. The special effects on pages 42–43 sound especially good on an electric guitar.

You have to be very careful not to make any mistakes on an electric guitar, as the amplifier makes them sound louder and clearer than on a classical or acoustic guitar.

The pick-ups convert the sound from the strings into electric signals.

RHYTHM PICK-UP

TREBLE PICK-UP

TONE CONTROL

VOLUME CONTROL

VOLUME CONTROL

TONE CONTROL

REVERB INPUT FOR ECHO EFFECT

INPUT FOR JACK LEAD

PICK-UP SELECTOR SWITCH

JACK LEAD

AMPLIFIER

Warning

A faulty amplifier can be very dangerous. Do not try and mend it yourself and always have it serviced by a qualified electrician. Make sure the plug for the amplifier has an earth.

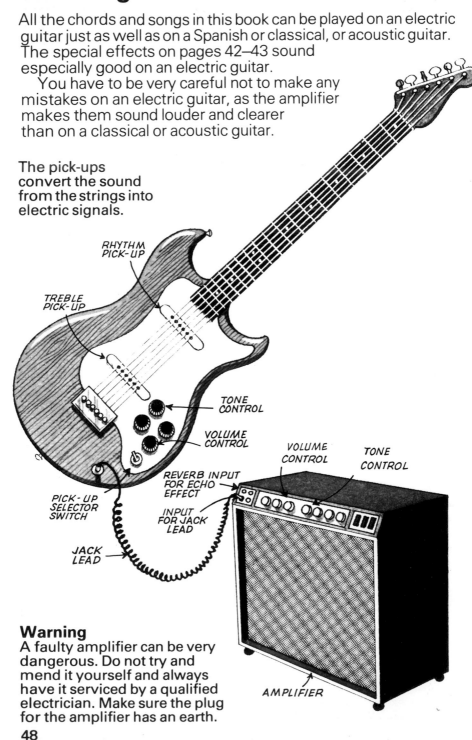

AMPLIFIER

Pick-ups

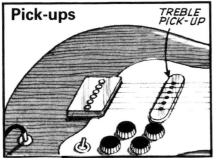

TREBLE PICK-UP

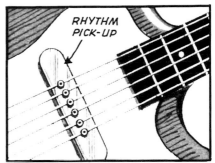

RHYTHM PICK-UP

You can choose which pick-up to use with the pick-up selector switch. The treble pick-up (nearest the bridge) gives a bright, hard sound.

The rhythm pick-up, the one nearest the neck of the guitar, gives a fuller sound. Some guitars also have a middle pick-up.

Strings

For each of the pick-ups there is a volume control knob and a tone control knob.

The strings come in four thicknesses, or gauges. Light gauge are best for solo lead guitar work and the heavier strings for a stronger bass sound.

Special effect pedals

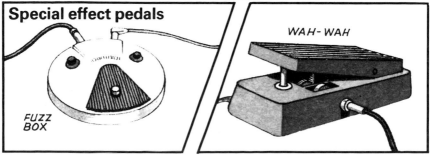

WAH-WAH

FUZZ BOX

A lot of the sounds on pop records are made by effect pedals which you plug in between the guitar and the

amplifier. A fuzz box makes the sound fuller and dirtier, and a wah-wah makes a crying effect as you pump the foot pedal.

Restringing a guitar

After a while, strings stretch and are difficult to tune. If you play your guitar a lot you should change all the strings about once every two months. You may even break a string occasionally.

If you have to replace one string, buy the right string for that note. Always use nylon strings on a classical or Spanish guitar – steel strings would warp the neck of the guitar.

Spanish or classical

To remove the old or broken string, turn the machine head anti-clockwise. Then pull the string out of the tuning peg and the bridge.

Push 3cm of the new string through the hole in the bridge from the sound hole side.

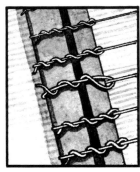

Wind the short end once round the rest of the string, then round itself, as shown above.*

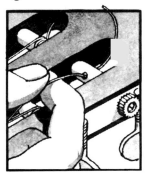

Pull the string tight and put the other end through the hole in the tuning peg.

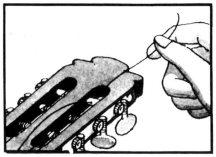

Pull the string through the hole but leave enough slack so you can tighten the string with the machine head.

To tighten the string, turn the machine head clockwise. Then tune the string to the correct note.

*If the string has an eyelet on the end, thread the other end through the eyelet and pull tight.

Steel-stringed guitars

Steel strings have a bead on the end which fits into the bridge. Some guitars have small pegs to hold the beads, on others, you thread the string through the bridge. Always remember to loosen the machine head before removing a string or it could lash out and cut you.

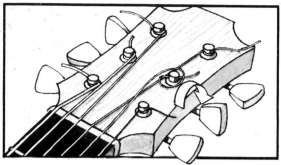

First, loosen the string by turning the machine head towards the neck of the guitar for bass strings and away from the neck for top strings.

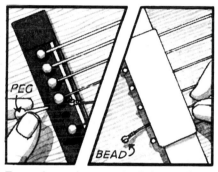

Free the other end of the string by pulling out the peg, if there is one, or threading the string out through the bridge.

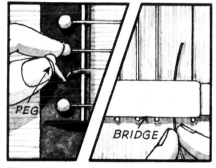

Fit the new string by putting the bead into the hole in the bridge and pushing in the peg, or by threading the string through the bridge towards the sound hole.

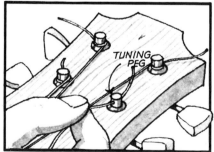

Thread the other end of the string through the tuning peg on the machine head, leaving enough slack to tighten the string with the machine head.

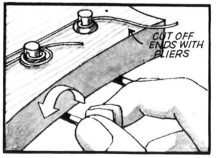

Tighten the machine head (away from the neck for bass strings and towards the neck for top strings). Then tune the string to the correct note.

How to read music

You can probably remember the tunes of a lot of songs and pick out the notes on the guitar or piano by ear. If you can read music, though, you can play tunes you have never heard before.

The notes

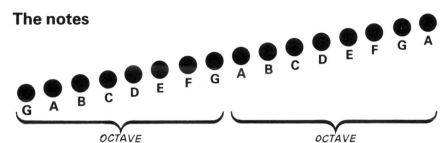

OCTAVE   OCTAVE

Each of the sounds which make up a tune is called a note and the notes are called by the letters of the alphabet. A sequence of eight notes going up or down in sound is called an octave.

How the notes are written

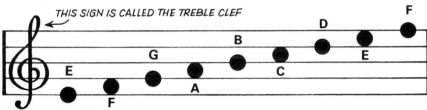

THIS SIGN IS CALLED THE TREBLE CLEF

Notes are written as circles on five lines called a stave. The position of each circle on the stave shows which note it is. To learn the notes, remember that the names of the notes between the lines spell the word "FACE", and the first letter of each word in the sentence "Every Good Boy Deserves Favours" gives the names of the notes on the lines of the stave.

Sharps and flats

SHARP   NATURAL

FLAT

PLAY A #

PLAY NORMAL A

Between most of the main notes there are half-notes called sharps and flats. A sharp (#) is half a note up and a flat (♭) is half a note down, so A# is the same as B♭.

The sharp or flat sign on the line for one of the notes at the beginning of a piece of music shows that you should play the sharp or flat of that note all through the music. The natural sign next to a note means you should play the ordinary note just that once.

How to find the notes on the guitar

This chart shows you how to find the notes on the guitar. The little charts above the notes show which string to press and the arrows show which string to pick for each note.

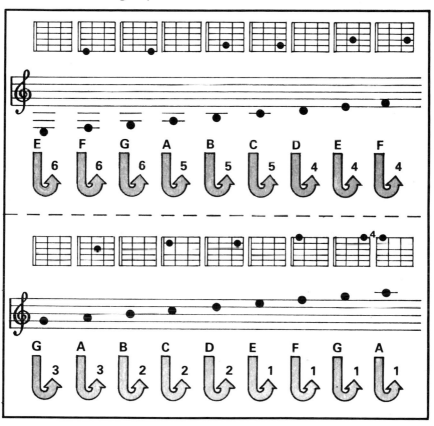

Timing

Semibreve	o	4 beats
Minim	d	2 beats
Crotchet	♩	1 beat
Quaver	♪	½ beat
Semiquaver	♪	¼ beat

Notes are written differently according to how many beats they last. For example, a crotchet lasts one beat and a quaver lasts for half a beat. A dot beside a note means you play it for half as long again – a crotchet with a dot lasts 1½ beats.

Rests

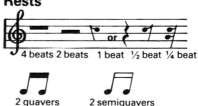

4 beats 2 beats 1 beat ½ beat ¼ beat

2 quavers   2 semiquavers

Several quavers or semiquavers together are joined by a line, as shown.

A rest sign shows that you should not play any note. The shape of the sign shows for how many beats you should not play.

Music for the songs

On the next five pages there is the music for each of the songs in this book. If you do not know one of the songs you can learn the tune from this music. The chart on page 53 shows how to find the notes on the guitar.

Mull of Kintyre

Chorus Mull of Kin - tyre O mist roll - ing in from the sea my de - sire is al - ways to be here O Mull of Kin - tyre.

1. Far have I trav - elled and much have I seen Dark dis - tant mountains with val - leys of green Past pain - ted des - erts the sun - sets on fire As he car - ries me home to the Mull of Kin - tyre.

2.
Smiles in the sunshine and tears in the rain
Carry me back where my mem'ries remain
Flickering embers grow higher and high'r
As they carry me back to the Mull of Kintyre.

3.
Sweep through the heather like deer in the glen
Carry me back to the days I knew then
Nights when we sang like a heavenly choir
Of the life and the times of the Mull of Kintyre.

McCartney/Laine © 1977 MPL Communications Ltd.
Used by permission of McCartney Music.

Sailing

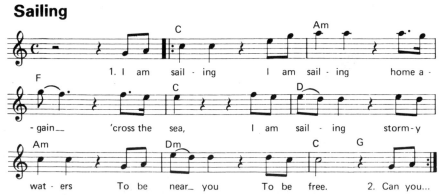

1. I am sail - ing I am sail - ing home a - gain 'cross the sea, I am sail - ing storm - y wat - ers To be near you To be free. 2. Can you...

Words and music by Gavin Sutherland © Island Music Ltd.
Used by permission of Island Music Ltd.

In the Summertime

1. In the sum-mer time, when the wea-ther is high, you can stretch right up an' tou-ch the sky, when the wea-ther's fine, you got wo-men, you got wo-men on your mind, Have a drink, have a drive go out an' see what you can find.

Words and music by Ray Dorset © Our Music Ltd.
Used by permission of Our Music Ltd.

Puff (the Magic Dragon)

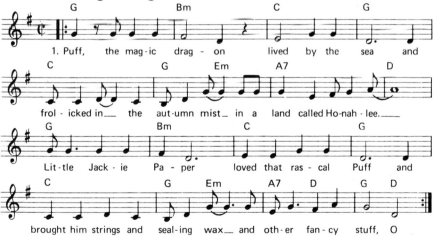

1. Puff, the mag-ic drag-on lived by the sea and frol-icked in the aut-umn mist in a land called Ho-nah-lee. Lit-tle Jack-ie Pa-per loved that ras-cal Puff and brought him strings and seal-ing wax and oth-er fan-cy stuff, O

2. Together they would travel on a boat with billowed sail
   Jackie kept a look-out perched on Puff's gigantic tail.
   Noble kings and princes would bow when-e'er he came
   And pirate ships would low'r their flag when Puff roared out his name, O

3. A dragon lives for ever, but not so little boys
   Painted wings and giant rings make way for other toys.
   One grey night it happened, Jackie Paper came no more
   And Puff that mighty dragon, he ceased his fearless roar, O

4. His head was bent in sorrow, green scales fell like rain
   Puff no longer went to play along the cherry lane.
   Without his lifelong friend Puff could not be brave
   So Puff that mighty dragon sadly slipped into his cave, O

Words and music by Peter Yarrow and Leonard Lipton
© Warner Bros Music. Used by permission of Warner Bros Music.

55

The House of the Rising Sun

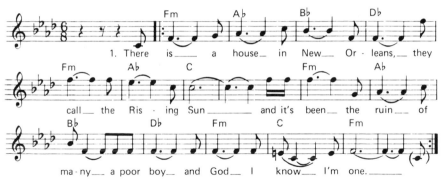

1. There is ___ a house___ in New___ Or - leans,___ they call___ the Ris - ing Sun ___ and it's been___ the ruin ___ of ma - ny___ a poor boy___ and God___ I know___ I'm one.___

2. My mother was a tailor, she sewed my new blue jeans
   My father was a gamblin' man, down in New Orleans.

3. Now the only thing a gambler needs is a suitcase and a trunk
   And the only time that he'll be satisfied is when he's all a - drunk.

4. O Mother tell your children not to do what I have done
   And spend your lives in sin and misery in the House of the Rising Sun.

5. I've got one foot on the platform, I've got the other foot on the train
   I'm going back to New Orleans to wear the ball and chain.

Traditional

Hotel California

1. On a dark de-sert high - way, cool wind in my hair Warm___ smell of Co - li - tas,___ ri - sing up through the air, ___ Up a - head in the dis - tance,___ I saw a shim - mer - ing light, my head grew heavy and my sight grew dim, ___ I had to stop for the night,___ 2. There she stood in the door - way,___

I heard the mis-sion bell___ and I was think-ing to my self___ this could be hea-ven or this could be hell,___ Then she lit up a can-dle,___ and she showed me the way, There were voi-ces down the cor-ri-dor,___ I thought I heard them say,___ Wel-come to the Ho-tel Cal-i-for-nia, such a love-ly place, (Such a love-ly place), such a love-ly face, Plen-ty of room at___ the Ho-tel Cal-i-for-nia, a-ny time___ of year (a-ny time___ of year), you can find___ it here.

Words and music by Don Felder, Don Henley and Glenn Frey
© Warner Bros Music. Used by permission of
Warner Bros Music.

Mr Tambourine Man

Hey! Mis-ter Tam-bou-rine Man play a song for me, I'm not sleep-y and there is no place I'm go-in' to._____ Hey! Mis-ter Tam-bou-rine Man play a song for me in the jin-gle jan-gle morn-in' I'll come fol-low-in' you._____ Though I know that eve-nin's em-pire has re-turned in-to sand, van-ished from my hand, left me blind-ly here to stand but still not sleep-in'._____ My wea-ri-ness a-maz-es me I'm bran-ded on my feet, I have no one to meet and the an-cient emp-ty street's too dead for dreamin'._____

Words and music by Bob Dylan © Warner Bros Music.
Used by permission of Warner Bros Music.

Michael Row the Boat Ashore

1. Mi-chael row the boat a shore, All-a-lu-ya, Mi-chael row the boat a-shore, All-a-lu_____ya, 2. Sis-ter

58   Traditional

Chord charts

If you play songs from guitar music and come across a chord you do not know, you can look it up on the next five pages. All the chords of one type, such as minor chords or major chords, are grouped together.

    If you find one particular chord very difficult to play, you need only finger and play the top four strings. Alternatively you can play another chord which sounds like it. For example, you can play a major chord instead of a sixth or seventh and a minor chord instead of a minor sixth or seventh. For chords called ninths, elevenths or thirteenths, you can play the seventh, or the major chord.

    The charts are the same as in the rest of this book – the first string is at the top and a small number on the left shows which fret the chart begins at. A cross next to a string means do not play that string.

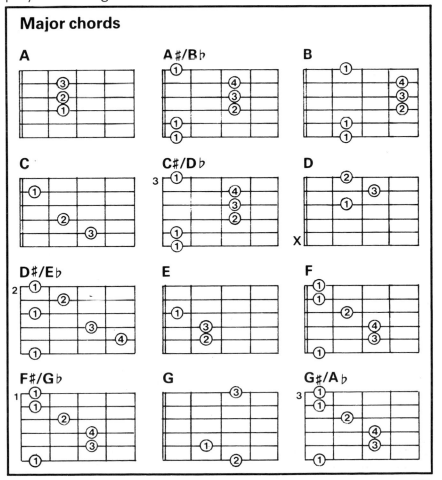

Major chords

A   A♯/B♭   B

C   C♯/D♭   D

D♯/E♭   E   F

F♯/G♭   G   G♯/A♭

Minor chords

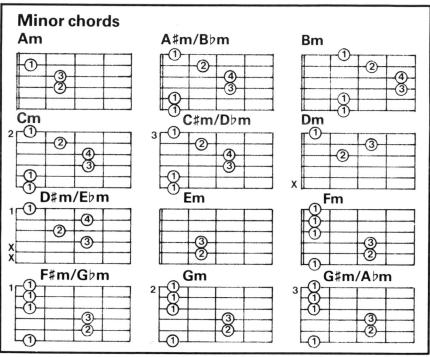

Am   A#m/B♭m   Bm

Cm   C#m/D♭m   Dm

D#m/E♭m   Em   Fm

F#m/G♭m   Gm   G#m/A♭m

Dominant 7th

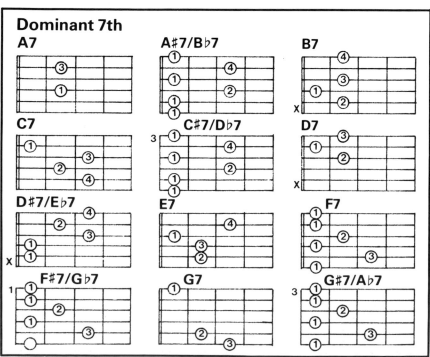

A7   A#7/B♭7   B7

C7   C#7/D♭7   D7

D#7/E♭7   E7   F7

F#7/G♭7   G7   G#7/A♭7

60

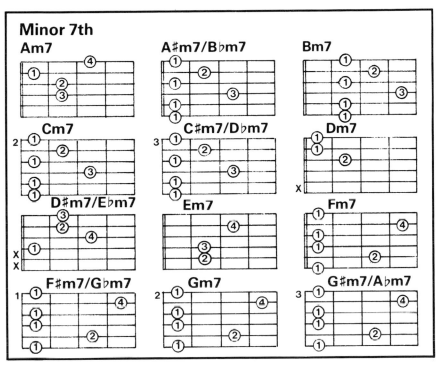

Minor 7th

Am7   A#m7/B♭m7   Bm7

Cm7   C#m7/D♭m7   Dm7

D#m7/E♭m7   Em7   Fm7

F#m7/G♭m7   Gm7   G#m7/A♭m7

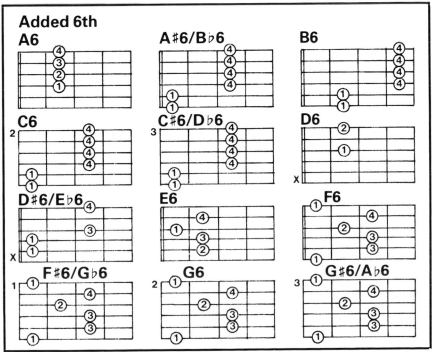

Added 6th

A6   A#6/B♭6   B6

C6   C#6/D♭6   D6

D#6/E♭6   E6   F6

F#6/G♭6   G6   G#6/A♭6

Minor 6th

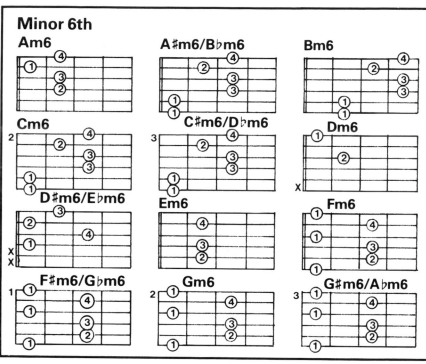

Am6 · A#m6/Bbm6 · Bm6 · Cm6 · C#m6/Dbm6 · Dm6 · D#m6/Ebm6 · Em6 · Fm6 · F#m6/Gbm6 · Gm6 · G#m6/Abm6

Major 7th

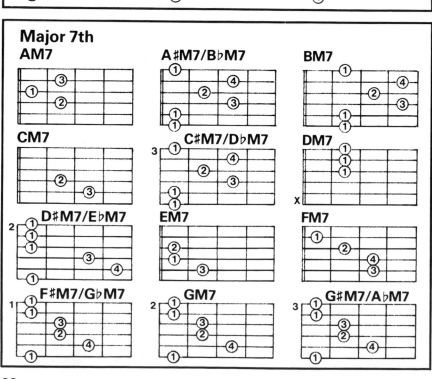

AM7 · A#M7/BbM7 · BM7 · CM7 · C#M7/DbM7 · DM7 · D#M7/EbM7 · EM7 · FM7 · F#M7/GbM7 · GM7 · G#M7/AbM7

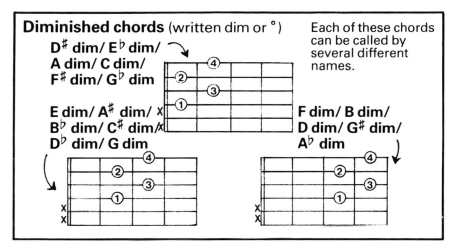

Diminished chords (written dim or °)

D# dim/ E♭ dim/
A dim/ C dim/
F# dim/ G♭ dim

E dim/ A# dim/
B♭ dim/ C# dim/
D♭ dim/ G dim

Each of these chords can be called by several different names.

F dim/ B dim/
D dim/ G# dim/
A♭ dim

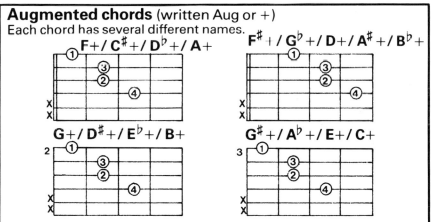

Augmented chords (written Aug or +)
Each chord has several different names.

F+/ C#+/ D♭+/ A+

F#+ / G♭+/ D+/ A#+/ B♭+

G+/ D#+/ E♭+/ B+

G#+ / A♭+ / E+/ C+

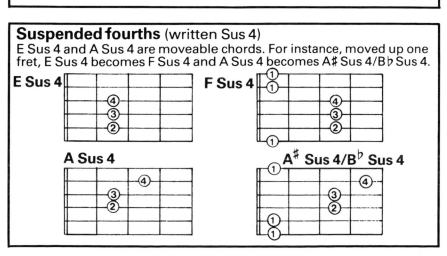

Suspended fourths (written Sus 4)
E Sus 4 and A Sus 4 are moveable chords. For instance, moved up one fret, E Sus 4 becomes F Sus 4 and A Sus 4 becomes A# Sus 4/B♭ Sus 4.

E Sus 4

F Sus 4

A Sus 4

A# Sus 4/B♭ Sus 4

Index